George Washington

★ ★

The Man Who Would Not Be King

George Washington
The Man Who Would Not Be King

Stephen Krensky

SCHOLASTIC INC.
New York Toronto London Auckland Sydney

Photo Credits

The American Museum of Natural History: p. 80; AP/Wide World: p. 62; Bettman Archive: pp. 20, 27, 32, 50, 57, 110; Chicago Historical Society: p. 67; Culver Pictures: p. 52; Library of Congress: p. 72; Kenneth M. Newman, The Old Print Shop, New York City: p. 40; the New York Public Library: pp. 2, 43; Northwind Pictures: p. 92; the Virginia Museum of Fine Arts: p. 88.

ISBN 0-590-43730-5

12 11 10 9 8 7 6 5   4 5 6/9

Printed in the U.S.A.   40

First Scholastic printing, January 1991

For Susie Perlman

Contents

George Washington
* *
The Man Who Would Not Be King

1
Early Years

The fields and valleys of eastern Virginia were dotted with small towns in the late winter of 1732. Some of the settlers were newly arrived from England. Others were descended from colonists who had been settling in Virginia since the landing at Jamestown in 1607.

Augustine Washington was the grandson of one such immigrant. Augustine, known as Gus, was a farmer and a justice of the peace. He built a grist mill and developed iron mines. His businesses were not always successful, but they kept him very busy.

His second wife, Mary, was busy, too. On February 22, she gave birth to a son. They named him George. Gus already had three children from

Young settlers in the colonial era.

a first wife who had died. Only his young daughter, Jane, lived with them. The older sons, Lawrence and Austin, were away at school in England.

The Washingtons lived in a little house on Pope's Creek, near the Potomac River. The house had four rooms and a chimney at each end. It wasn't large or fancy. When baby George cried for food or attention, he could clearly be heard in all four rooms at once.

Little George, however, was not the baby of the family for long. A new sister, Betty, was born before his second birthday, and a brother, Samuel, before his third. Sadly, his half sister, Jane, died after a brief illness before George could really get to know her.

The growing family soon moved to a larger farmhouse near Little Hunting Creek, about forty miles further up the Potomac. The extra room didn't last for long, though. In the next few years, two more brothers were born — Jack and Charles — and the house was full again.

When George was six, the family moved once more, this time to the Ferry farm, across the Rappahannock River from Fredericksburg. At this point the Washingtons could afford to build a larger home. The main house had six rooms, four on the first floor and two on the second. There were thirteen beds in all, filled every night with large and small Washingtons, as well as with occasional guests.

The kitchen was in a separate building out back. This was put there for safety. Colonial kitchens could be dangerous places. The hot fires roasting meats or baking breads sometimes escaped the hearth and burned down the house.

In the barn, horses, cows, and chickens were kept. The farm raised almost all its own food. Farmhands and slaves took care of most things, but a small boy like George could help feed the chickens and milk the cow.

Nearby Fredericksburg was probably the first town George had ever seen. It had several houses and buildings all close together. One general store sold everything from gunpowder to pots and pans. At the large dock on the river, large and small ships sailed in, including some that had crossed the Atlantic. Fredericksburg wasn't a city like Williamsburg, the capital of Virginia, where 2,000 people including the royal governor lived, but it must have looked pretty big to George.

In 1738, George's half brother Lawrence returned from school in England. Lawrence had never met George. The long journey from England to Virginia was not one that a schoolboy took very often. Lawrence was twenty now, and six-year-old George was very excited to meet him. Lawrence was pleased, too. He was intelligent and kind, and very fond of George. Unfortunately, the two half brothers didn't get to spend too much time together.

Before long Lawrence enlisted with a colonial

regiment serving with the British Navy, which was fighting the Spanish in the Caribbean. His new officer's uniform was very impressive. It probably made George wish for a uniform of his own with brass buttons and a cocked hat.

While Lawrence was off doing his duty, young George spent his time getting an education. Some years he rode ten miles to reach a one-room school for children of many ages. He learned to read and write when he was seven, but he never did much reading for pleasure. He preferred arithmetic.

He also practiced writing with a quill. Good penmanship was a sign of a gentleman, and George's was neat and elegant. One of his exercises was copying 110 sayings under the title "Rules of Civility and Decent Behavior in Company and Conversation." Among these guidelines was *If you cough, sneeze, sigh or yawn, do it not loud, but privately.* . . . Another cautionary note was to *Kill no vermin in the sight of others.*

George did not copy these sayings just to improve his penmanship. Colonial children were expected to act like small adults. They wore miniature versions of adult clothes — waistcoats and knee breeches for boys, petticoats and bodices for girls — and were sternly taught how to behave in public. George learned these lessons well. He had a serious and honest nature. He was always proper and a little stiff around people. His big hands and feet always seemed to get in his way, and he was never good at telling jokes.

Still, George and the other colonial children managed to have some fun. There were occasional country fairs, complete with races and puppet shows. George probably flew kites on windy afternoons and rolled hoops with his brothers and sister. He may have played leapfrog and hide-and-seek. In the summer he could swim in the river. When he was eight or nine, he probably got a flintlock rifle and began learning how to shoot and hunt.

In 1742, George's half brother Austin returned from school in England, too. Like both his half brothers, George expected to complete his education there. But his father died the next year, in April of 1743, leaving George's mother in charge. Mary Ball Washington had no intention of sending her oldest son 3,000 miles away from her reach. He might not dress warmly enough. Or eat properly. And besides, she needed his attention at home. No, one thing was clear. George was going to stay right where he was.

2
The Young Surveyor

The death of George's father was not only a sad event; it changed his life in many ways. His half brothers Lawrence and Austin inherited land on which they planned to build their own homes. At age eleven, George remained at the Ferry farm with his mother. According to his father's will, he would inherit the farm and ten slaves on his twenty-first birthday. The farm and the slaves were treated the same — both were considered property. The economics of a Virginia plantation relied on the availability of slave labor. Most people in the colony took the notion of slavery for granted, even though they opposed other forms of unfair captivity.

For the moment, though, George's inheritance was in his mother's hands. Mary Washington was concerned about George's future, but mostly in terms of how it would affect her. She had a rather narrow view of life. Orphaned at a young age, she had spent many years fending for herself. Now, after twelve years of marriage, her husband was dead. Although she was only thirty-five and in excellent health, she worried a lot. In her eyes, George must always see to her needs first. This attitude did not foster a close bond between them. George was a polite and dutiful son, but he squirmed under his mother's gaze and longed to escape from it.

George took every chance to visit Lawrence and Austin. Austin lived a comfortable life, mostly out of public view. Lawrence, though, was on his way to becoming an important man in Virginia politics. With his fine manners and habits, he fit in comfortably with the highest ranks of Virginia society. His marriage to Anne Fairfax, daughter of Colonel William Fairfax, also raised his standing. The colonel's cousin, Lord Fairfax, had huge land holdings in Virginia, and Colonel Fairfax looked after them.

The Fairfaxes liked George, and he spent much time at their brick country estate, Belvoir. He spent even more time at the new home Lawrence had built. Lawrence named it Mount Vernon in honor of Admiral Edward Vernon, under whom he had served in the navy.

At Mount Vernon and Belvoir, George mingled with a sophisticated and educated group of peo-

Mount Vernon.

ple. Lawrence, like other well-placed men of Virginia, mixed his business with public service. George learned from his example. There were also other, less serious, lessons to be learned. George went fox hunting, he played cards, and he developed a taste for expensive clothing.

Meanwhile, his education proceeded in fits and starts. George's spelling was passable. He studied geography and he read some classics. His favorite subject was mathematics. He knew algebra and trigonometry, and he enjoyed surveying. In his early teens, in fact, he surveyed his own fields for practice.

When he wasn't measuring his fields, George was learning what went into them. Much of the Virginia farmland was given over to growing tobacco, and George studied how it was done. He was interested in farming in the same methodical way that he liked mathematics. He respected the land because it stood a good chance of providing him with a decent income.

Lawrence had the thought, however, that George should try a career in the British Navy. The Fairfaxes were willing to use their influence to help him secure a position. George liked the idea. It was not the navy itself that appealed to him — he was indifferent to boats — so much as the prospect for adventure.

Either way, his mother objected. As his guardian, the final decision was hers. She was not yet prepared to let George leave her side. Extended visits with his brothers were one thing. Going off to sea for years at a time was something else.

That didn't mean George wasn't going to travel at all. In a time when many people never left their birthplace, George was eager to stretch his long legs. His first opportunity came after Lord Fairfax himself arrived from England in 1747. Lord Fairfax had inherited a huge piece of land — five million acres — stretching from Virginia's Westmoreland County westward into the mountains. For many years there had been a question of who actually controlled this land. Indian claims, as well as those of other colonies, had needed to be settled in court. This had taken many years. Now that it was done,

Lord Fairfax wanted the land surveyed.

In 1748, a survey team was assembled. Colonel Fairfax's son, George William, was going along to represent the Fairfaxes on the expedition. Sixteen-year-old George Washington, George William's good friend, was going along to keep him company.

The journey began in March, and George kept a diary of his adventures. It was his first trip of this kind, and many things were new to him.

Tuesday 15th. We set out early . . . & Worked hard till Night & Then returnd to Penningtons. We got our Suppers & was lighted into a Room & I not being so good a Woodsman as the rest of my Company I striped my self very orderly & went into the Bed as they call'd it when to my Surprize I found it to be nothing but a Little Straw Matted together without Sheets or any thing else but only one Thread Bear blanket with double its Weight of Vermin such as Lice Fleas &c. I was glad to get up (as soon as the Light was carried from us) & put on my cloths & Lay as my Companions. Had we not been very tired I am sure we should not have slep'd much that night. . . .

In a month of traveling, the two Georges met Indians, forded rivers swollen with winter snow, saw rattlesnakes, traveled by canoe, and watched their tent carried off one night in a strong wind. It was quite a change from their usually comfortable lives.

Whatever surveying knowledge George gained on the trip, he learned even more about land speculation. The Washingtons, like many colonial farming families, believed that the road to wealth was through land. The idea was simple enough, although it required enterprise and foresight. When settlements were first established, large pieces of land went to well-connected people — rich investors or friends of the king. But beyond the boundaries of these settlements was wilderness. The land there would be valuable someday, but only after the original settlement expanded. Of course, some parts of this wilderness would be more valuable than others. Anyone who took the trouble to stake out a promising claim might someday profit greatly by it.

At seventeen George became a surveyor. It seemed like a natural development. He was precise, he liked working with numbers, and he was interested in land development. In 1749, he helped lay out the new town of Alexandria and became the county surveyor of Culpeper County. He also did more surveying for Lord Fairfax in the Shenandoah Valley.

George kept busy surveying, and he turned a profit doing it. He used the money to buy well-sited wilderness land. George had a good eye for evaluating the countryside, and he was confident his purchases would increase in value.

His time in the wilderness gave George valuable experience. There were no stores where he could buy food, or comfortable inns where he could spend the night. He had to hunt for his suppers and build whatever shelters he needed. As a result, he became an experienced frontiersman, and was as accustomed to camping out in the woods as he was to dancing at a formal Virginia ball.

The only shadow in George's life fell on his brother Lawrence. Lawrence was not well. He had a hacking cough that wouldn't go away. Twice he traveled to London to see doctors, but there was nothing they could do for him. In 1751 he decided to spend the winter in Barbados. Perhaps the hot climate would help dry out his lungs. George went along to keep his brother company.

They had a busy time socially on the island, at least until George caught smallpox. Luckily, his case was relatively mild. The disease left his face pockmarked, but otherwise his good health returned.

Lawrence's cough, though, worsened. As winter passed, he decided to go to Bermuda. The air there might be good for him. George, however, had business waiting for him in Virginia, and returned home.

In mid-June, 1752, Lawrence finally came home to Mount Vernon. Unfortunately, the changes of location had not helped. He was near death. He

13

spent the next few weeks settling his affairs. On July 26, he died, leaving George executor of his estate. When Lawrence's daughter Sarah died two months later, George leased Mount Vernon from Lawrence's widow, Anne, who then moved away. Upon her death the estate would become his.

3
A Taste of War

At the age of twenty in 1752, George Washington was tall and broad-shouldered, with reddish-brown hair and blue eyes. He now controlled a fine estate and enjoyed a rising social position. But George was not satisfied. He was ambitious enough to want some power and responsibilities outside the borders of Mount Vernon.

His brother Lawrence had been the commanding officer of Virginia's militia. George wanted that job for himself. He was fourteen years younger than Lawrence and had absolutely no military experience, but these were just details to George. He was a very confident young man.

His campaign for the post was a partial success. The governor decided to divide Virginia into four military districts, and George was put in charge of one of them. He was almost twenty-one when he entered Virginia's militia as Major George Washington.

The post paid one hundred pounds a year, a good sum of money. Major Washington was supposed to earn it by traveling through the district, teaching the country militia officers how to drill their men. The traveling part was easy; the new major rode a horse well. But Washington had never done any drilling before. Somehow he managed, though, or at least nobody complained.

His responsibilities became more serious in the fall of 1753. At that point, France and England were resting between one of their many wars. However, even during these so-called peacetimes, one country or the other was usually up to something.

The French were currently building forts between Lake Erie and the Allegheny River. The land under these forts was claimed by both Pennsylvania and Virginia. Either way it was English land, which was no place for a French fort to be.

This French activity troubled Governor Dinwiddie of Virginia. As the governor, he was naturally anxious about any possible French threat to Virginia colonists. As a private citizen, Dinwiddie was also a member of the Ohio Company, a business group that speculated in and developed land grants. Other founding members were George's half brothers Lawrence and Augustine. Obviously, English land grants near these French forts would be worthless if the French controlled the land itself.

Dinwiddie decided to tell the French they must either leave the area or risk war. To deliver this message he needed a special messenger. This would not be a comfortable journey made in the back of a coach. The messenger would need to cross over 500 wilderness miles in the face of winter.

Washington volunteered at once. The risks and the dangers mattered little to him. This was a chance to prove himself. He received his orders on October 31, 1753, and started out the same day. His party included an interpreter, an expert scout, and four experienced Indian traders.

The journey was long and unpleasant. Bad weather followed the messenger and his companions. In his diary, Washington mentioned "excessive Rains and vast Quantity of Snow." It took six weeks for his company to reach Fort-le-Boeuf, twenty miles south of Lake Erie, where Washington delivered Dinwiddie's message.

The French commander was not impressed.

Washington could do nothing more. He had delivered the warning, and the French had chosen to ignore it. Knowing the governor would want this news as soon as possible, Washington and the others set out for home immediately. Unfortunately, the horses had trouble traveling through the deep December snow. Finally, Washington and the scout, Christopher Gist, went ahead on foot. Washington wrote in his journal what happened next:

The Day following . . . we fell in with a Party of French Indians, who had lain in Wait for us; one of them fired at Mr. Gist or me, not 15 Steps, but fortunately missed. We took this fellow into Custody, and kept him till about 9 o'Clock at Night, and then let him go, and walked all the remaining Part of the Night without making any Stop, that we might get . . . out of the reach of their Pursuit the next Day, as we were well assured they would follow our Tract as soon as it was light . . . .

After two more days Washington and Gist reached the Monongahela River. They were hoping the wide river would be frozen over, so that they could simply walk across it. Instead, they found the river filled with ice floes rushing along in the current.

In a hurry to continue their journey, they built a raft and attempted to cross anyway. When the raft got caught in the ice, Washington tried to push it away with a long pole. The ice shifted suddenly, and he was thrown into the water. Eventually he managed to pull himself back onto the raft, where his wet clothes soon froze. He and Gist abandoned their raft for an island in the middle of the river. There they spent a truly miserable night in the cold. The next morning, the top of the river was a sheet of ice, and they could walk over it easily.

On January 16, 1754, Washington reached Williamsburg and made his written report to Governor Dinwiddie. He wrote of his adventures with a cool detachment that caught the governor's attention. Dinwiddie had the account printed and widely distributed. In a few days, young Major Washington was the talk of the colony. It was his first taste of fame.

Meanwhile, Dinwiddie remained very concerned. Both his investment and certain settlers were still in danger from the French. Some members of his Ohio Company had established a base at the forks of the Ohio River. Dinwiddie wanted to make sure that this base remained in British control.

In April, Washington led a new expedition of about 160 men to secure this base. But they were too late. On the way there they met thirty-three members of the Ohio Company returning from the forks. These men reported that a thousand French soldiers and Indians had arrived at their little base not long before. The thirty-three men stood no chance against such a force, so they had quickly surrendered. Happily, they had not been killed. The French had simply sent them home.

Unwilling to leave the French unchallenged in the area, Washington went on. More men were sent to join his expedition until they numbered about 350 in all. About forty miles from the

French position, Washington had his men construct a crude fort, which he called Fort Necessity. From this base he surprised an advance force of thirty Frenchmen, ten of whom were killed. The rest were taken prisoner. There was a problem, though. This French group had papers stating that they were on a peaceful mission, similar to the one Washington had undertaken months earlier. Only now it was the French who were warning the British to keep their distance.

Washington waved aside these diplomatic details. He thought the French had been attacking them, and that was enough to justify his actions. Besides, he had other things to think about. The

Standing watch at Fort Necessity.

main French force moving against him was three times the size of his own. This army soon surrounded the fort.

It shortly became clear that Fort Necessity would have been more aptly named Fort Miscalculation. Too small to effectively protect the army, it was also vulnerable from higher ground. Only two things saved Washington's expedition from being totally wiped out. The first was that colonial rifles, whether French or English, were very inaccurate. The other was that in mid-afternoon it rained, making it difficult for anyone's guns to fire at all.

Even so, one hundred of Washington's men were dead or wounded. All of the ammunition was soaked. Supplies were low, and water was collecting in the trenches. Nevertheless, Washington refused to surrender.

His stubbornness was rewarded at nightfall. The French could easily have asked for an unconditional surrender. Instead, they let Washington off the hook. They insisted that they had been only avenging the attack on their diplomatic force. If Washington would sign a document taking responsibility for that attack, and tell the British that the land belonged to the French, he and the remainder of his men could go home in peace.

On July 4, 1754, Washington signed. It seemed that he had bravely wriggled off a very sharp hook. First he had won a victory, and then he had held off a much larger force until terms could be agreed on. At least that's how it looked to his countrymen back home in Virginia.

The truth was very different. In the first place, Washington had placed his fort poorly. This decision, coupled with his later surrender, made the British look foolish. In the coming war, many Indians would become French allies because the British colonists seemed so incompetent here. The British leaders in England probably were mumbling a bit about incompetence, too. They were not pleased that an officer representing them had taken the blame for the murder of some French diplomats.

Unaware of these views, Washington hoped to transfer from his colonial command to the regular British Army. But when his regiment was dispersed, he learned differently. No colonist would be offered any high rank in a transfer.

Angry and disappointed, Washington resigned his commission. But the excitement of battle had stirred him. As he wrote, "I have heard the bullets whistle; and believe me, there is something charming in the sound."

Washington was not out of uniform for long. The British still wanted to drive the French from their forts in colonial territory. The next year, 1755, British General Edward Braddock invited Washington to join his expedition to take Fort Duquesne from the French.

Braddock's army moved very slowly through

the wilderness. Trappers or explorers could pass quickly over ancient paths or make do with no paths at all. But armies, traveling with heavy cannon, supply wagons, and other goods, needed roads to go anywhere, and they had to build them first. On many days the army moved only a couple of miles.

On June 20, Washington became sick with fever and stayed behind at a supply depot. For a few days he could do nothing but lie in bed as the army marched on. But Washington was upset at the thought of missing out on the coming battle. As soon as he was well enough to travel (but not well enough to ride a horse), he commandeered a wagon and tried to catch up with General Braddock. Washington reached him on July 8, when the army was just a few miles from Fort Duquesne.

The next afternoon the French and Indians attacked the British camp. Although the enemy force was smaller, their ambush was very effective. They made good use of the land, kneeling under bushes and ducking behind trees. The British soldiers, accustomed to fighting in orderly patterns on open fields, didn't know what to do. While they hesitated in confusion, their red coats made easy targets. Many of them died before making up their minds.

General Braddock gamely tried to rally his men, but he had no training for such a situation. He fought bravely, but was soon killed.

Washington was leading the relatively cool-headed Virginia regiment. They had the most experience fighting such battles, and they didn't panic. But they could not lead the British to victory. There were too few of them, and too many British soldiers had already died.

Under the circumstances, Washington coolly ordered the army to fall back. His orders made the retreat far more successful than it would have been otherwise. Meanwhile he stayed in the forefront of battle. The men around him marveled that he escaped injury. Four bullets whistled through his coat. Two horses were shot out from under him. And yet the colonel himself remained unharmed. Was this pure luck, or the hand of Fate? Whatever it was, the men were glad that Colonel Washington was on their side.

4
Gentleman Farmer

Washington had now reached the ripe old age of twenty-six. The colonial world of 1758 put much stock in first impressions, and Washington had a way about him that people often noticed. As one friend described him in a letter, Washington was "six feet two inches in his stockings and weigh[ed] 175 pounds. . . . In conversation, he looks you full in the face, is deliberate, deferential, and engaging. His demeanor at all times composed and dignified. . . ."

Dignified or not, Washington was clearly blocked from getting a high commission in the British Regular Army. As a colonial officer, he did not have the right political connections. He might have climbed slowly through the ranks, but his pride and ambition were not willing to wait.

So Washington resigned his commission. He had done his duty and then some. It was time to turn his attention to other things. Although military matters had dominated Washington's life during the past few years, he found some time for other pursuits. While at Mount Vernon and on trips to Williamsburg, he attended many parties, mingling with the best of Virginia society.

He also discovered the attractions of girls. George was not a witty speaker, but he wrote several girls romantic letters and poems. He probably received similar notes in return. Of all the young women he met, Sally Fairfax, the wife of his friend, George William, made the greatest impression. She was charming and clever, and George was quite taken with her. She seemed to encourage his attentions, yet kept their friendship proper and discreet.

There were other women in whom George was interested. One, Elizabeth Fauntleroy, he actually tried to court twice. She, however, was not interested either time in such a serious and practical young man, and married someone else.

But seriousness and practicality could be attractive, too. Among those who valued these traits was Martha Dandridge Custis. She was five feet tall with light brown hair and hazel eyes. Born June 21, 1731, Martha came from a modest background. She was not known for her clever wit or her beauty, but she was sensible, clear-headed, and unassuming. Her first marriage, to

Martha Dandridge Custis, later to become Martha Washington.

John Custis, a wealthy planter, had vaulted Martha into high society. Custis, though, had died young, leaving Martha with two young children and a large fortune.

Martha had taken charge of the family estate with great care. She was not well-educated, but she did have good judgment. She searched out business advice when she needed it, and trusted her own common sense much of the time.

No doubt these traits appealed to Colonel Washington. During the spring of 1758 he made several short visits to Martha's home. It was time for him to be thinking of marriage, and the young widow, Mrs. Custis, would make a very proper and suitable wife.

Love and marriage did not always go hand in hand in colonial America. Men and women often lacked a wide choice of partners to choose from, and practical matters were considered more important than romantic ones. George never fell in love with Martha. His boyhood crush on Sally Fairfax remained in his heart, although it was a love confined to his letters. For her part, Martha probably didn't fall in love with George, either. She recognized that he would manage her estate well, and responsibly care for her two young children.

Their marriage was celebrated on January 6, 1759, in one of Martha's homes. It was called the "White House" by her family. George wore a fine new blue velvet suit, while Martha wore a white brocaded silk dress and purple satin slippers. The wedding was not large, although several prominent guests attended from different parts of Virginia.

The marriage was fairly happy to begin with and became more so over time. Martha was cheerful and kind; she made a good companion. She was "a quiet wife, a quiet soul," in George's words. He meant it as a compliment.

To make room for his new family, Washington added another story to Mount Vernon. He adjusted not only to being a husband, but to being a stepfather, too. John Parke Custis and Martha Parke Custis, known as Jackie and Patsy, were only four and two at the time of the wedding. Martha, who was sensible about most things, spoiled her children terribly. George, who became their guardian, followed her lead. He was fond of the children in his own way. He bought them many toys and treats and expensive clothes from London. It was not his nature, though, to play with them much in their make-believe games or share their secrets, so he remained a somewhat formal figure to them.

After spending six years going off to war and looking for adventure, Washington could have found life on the farm rather dull. But he didn't. In fact, he enjoyed being a country squire. On a typical summer morning, Washington would rise at dawn to make the rounds of his different farms. He was fascinated by everything that made his estates work. Mount Vernon was almost like a town by itself. In addition to the barns, stables, and henhouses, there was a flour mill, a smithy, and a spinning and weaving house. Beyond them, slave quarters and other cottages dotted the landscape. There were herds of horses and cattle, flocks of sheep, and many pigs.

Washington worked hard all day. At night there was almost always company for dinner. Relatives or friends were constantly coming to visit. Sometimes they stayed for months.

Running an estate had its successes and failures, but Washington took them in stride. He didn't waste his time shaking his fists against such forces of nature as droughts or floods or severe storms. On the other hand, he became increasingly angry with human forces — in this case, London merchants — whom he thought were taking advantage of him.

At this time in Virginia, almost all finished goods came from England. Raw resources — cotton, furs, timber — might originate in the colonies, but they were always processed across the sea. Raw cotton, for example, was sent to England to be turned into cloth, and then sold back to the colonists at a nice profit for the English manufacturers.

Had these goods been of fine quality, the colonists probably wouldn't have grumbled as much. But they weren't. London merchants often took advantage of their colonial customers. After all, it was tempting to send expensive yet inferior-quality merchandise to customers who lived 3,000 miles away. They could hardly walk into the shops and complain. And the merchants knew that most colonists wouldn't be able to wait for shoddy merchandise to be replaced, or incorrect orders to be refilled. They would take what they got and make do with it.

Like many others, Washington was a victim of this practice. However, he did not accept it quietly. In a letter to his London agents, he wrote:

. . . you may believe me when I tell you that instead of getting things good and fashionable . . . we often have Articles sent Us that coud only have been usd by our Forefathers in the days of yore. 'Tis a custom, I have some Reason to believe, with many Shop keepers, and Tradesmen in London, when they know Goods are bespoke for Exportation to palm sometimes old, and sometimes very slight and indifferent goods upon Us. . . .

While Washington was unhappy with the quality of the goods he purchased, he was also concerned about their cost. Even though he was the sole owner of Mount Vernon and was managing the large estate Martha brought to their marriage, Washington could not keep them out of debt. Fine clothes and food, new coaches, and — most of all — mediocre harvests, were costing him dearly.

Washington was growing tobacco over much of his farmland because that's what Virginia's larger landowners generally did. It was easy to raise, and good crops were very valuable. Admittedly, tobacco crops wore out the soil quickly, but many planters ignored this fact.

Washington did not. In truth, much of his land was ill-suited for growing tobacco. He did notice, though, that farmers with smaller holdings were doing well growing wheat, flax, and other crops instead of tobacco. These crops didn't need to be shipped to London. They were sold locally.

Washington understood the advantages of knowing his customers. If he changed his crops, he would no longer be at the mercy of London middlemen whom he hadn't met and didn't trust.

Tobacco farmers bringing their harvest to market.

Once Washington made up his mind, he set to work making a switch. He ordered books on agriculture, and he experimented with different fertilizers. Wheat became his primary crop, and he rotated his crops in a complicated system. The results were encouraging, and over the next few years his debts eased. But Washington would always remember how close he came to financial ruin because of the men in faraway London.

As busy as he was at Mount Vernon, Washington still found some time to travel. As a member of the House of Burgesses, the legislature of Virginia, he traveled about one hundred miles to Williamsburg several times a year when it met. He also made several trips west and south, sometimes for weeks at a time, to scout tracts of land he might wish to buy. The acquisition of land was more than a hobby for him. He was raised in an atmosphere that looked upon land ownership as the best road to long-term wealth. His father, grandfather, and great-grandfather had all improved their situations in this way. George was following their example. By the end of 1758, he increased his holdings to 9,381 acres. This was quite a change from the single farm he had inherited from his father.

At this point, Washington probably imagined he would spend the rest of his life as a comfortable landowner. His life was ordered and settled, prosperous, and just a little predictable. What could possibly disturb it now?

5
Taxation Without Representation

While Washington was minding his estates, the face of colonial America was changing. In 1700, the colonial population was 250,000. By 1750, it had grown to 1,500,000. Boston, New York, Philadelphia, and Charleston were bustling ports engaged in trade with many parts of the world.

The world of the colonists was becoming increasingly American — which reflected a change in colonial thinking. One hundred years earlier, American colonists had thought of themselves as English. After all, they had been born and raised in England. But time had passed. Although English laws and customs remained, many current colonists did not look to England with the same emotional ties as their parents or grandparents had. And new arrivals from other countries had no ties to England at all.

Politically, these differences remained in the background while everyone's attention was focused on wars with the French. Then, in 1763, the French and English stopped fighting. The French were the losers in this latest war, and their settlement was a costly one. In this Treaty of Paris, France gave up all its claims in Canada, in the Great Lakes, and in the upper Mississippi. That meant French soldiers would be leaving these lands forever.

Wars are expensive, even for the winners. The British government wanted to refill its treasury, and a good place to do that, the British ministers decided, was in America. The colonists were certainly going to benefit from the terms of the new treaty. Now they would pay for their peace of mind.

This payment came in the form of fees and taxes. The Navigation Acts, already in effect, became more strictly enforced. These acts pressured colonial merchants to transport their goods only in British ships, export certain things — such as tobacco, sugar, and furs — only to England, and buy imported goods only from English merchants. The whole idea was to force colonial business through British channels as much as possible. The plan worked well, but it frustrated American merchants who knew better deals were available elsewhere.

While the British government was regulating

colonial trade, it was also confining colonial expansion. King George III issued the Proclamation of 1763, which banned settlements west of the Appalachian Mountains. This decree aimed to keep colonists from further encroaching on Indian lands. The settlement of these lands had already led to a number of skirmishes between Indians and colonists. Just as important, though, the ban would keep colonists from moving westward beyond the reach of British control.

The proclamation upset many colonists. Even Washington, still a loyal British subject, didn't like it. In the past the government had always encouraged and benefited from the development of new lands. Abruptly halting this policy without consulting any colonial representatives seemed high-handed, even for a king.

Washington did not take the proclamation too seriously, though. As he wrote to a friend:

> . . . I can never look upon that Proclamation in any other light (but this I say between ourselves) than as a temporary expedient to quiet the Minds of the Indians & must fall of course in a few years especially when those Indians are consenting to our Occupying the Lands.

Washington did not explain why the Indians would willingly consent to the colonists occupying their lands. But he was satisfied it would happen.

King George III.

In 1765 another new act appeared. It required the purchase of stamps for printed documents such as wills and mortgages. This Stamp Act made a lot of people angry. Once again the colonists were not consulted. Why, they were not even represented in the British Parliament where these decisions were made. The idea of taxation without representation was very troubling.

George Washington was aware of the unrest. In sessions of Virginia's House of Burgesses, many representatives made strong speeches of protest. Washington's reaction was less dramatic. As he wrote to his wife's uncle:

. . . The Stamp Act Imposed on the Colonies . . . engrosses the conversation of the Speculative part of the Colonists, who look upon this

unconstitutional method of Taxation as a dire-
ful attack upon their Liberties, and loudly ex-
claim against the Violation. What may be the
result of this and some other (I think I may
add) ill judgd Measures, I will not undertake to
determine. . . .

Basically, Washington expected the British
government to see the error of its ways. Surely
its ministers could not be so shortsighted as all
that.

Or maybe they could. In 1767, the Townshend
Acts created new taxes on imports of tea, paper,
glass, and paint. The actions of the British government were beginning to remind Washington
of his problems with London merchants years
before. He didn't like being taken advantage of
then, and he liked it no better now. Washington
was a fair man, but he was fair to himself as well
as to other people. It certainly was convenient for
the British Parliament to tax the colonies without
giving them any say in the matter. But it wasn't
right.

Many colonists wanted to resist these new
taxes. Washington now became one of them. As
he wrote to his neighbor, George Mason, in 1769:

At a time when our lordly Masters in Great
Britain will be satisfied with nothing less than
the deprivation of American freedom, it seems
highly likely that some thing shou'd be done to

avert the stroke and maintain the liberty which
we have derived from our Ancestors. . . .

But what should the *some thing* be? Washington firmly believed that armed rebellion should be avoided if possible. Commercial warfare, though, was another matter. In May 1769, Washington strongly supported a resolution in the House of Burgesses stating that only it had the right to create taxes in Virginia. The royal governor promptly condemned the measure, but Washington did not change his mind.

These were not decisions to be made lightly. After all, Washington had a lot at stake in any confrontation with England. He was no footloose adventurer without family or property. Should there be a fight, and should he choose the wrong side to fight on, he could lose his lands — or even his life.

Meanwhile the incidents of violence were mounting. On March 5, 1770, a false fire alarm in Boston drew a large crowd into the street. Someone threw snowballs at one of the British soldiers nearby. He called for help. Another soldier was knocked down. As the crowd moved closer, the soldiers fired their muskets. Five people were killed.

This event, which came to be called the Boston Massacre, was followed in 1773 by the Boston Tea Party. To protest a tax on tea, colonists dressed up as Indians and dumped a cargo of tea from

The Boston Tea Party.

some ships into Boston Harbor. By the summer of 1774, new British edicts closed Boston Harbor (until colonists there paid for the ruined tea) and authorized the stationing of British troops in any colonial town.

These "Intolerable Acts," as they were called in America, fueled the talk of rebellion. It was no longer a hushed topic confined to the back tables of taverns. It was discussed openly and with great emotion. For Loyalists — people whose loyalty to England did not waver — the situation was becoming very uncomfortable. Some of them, including George William and Sally Fairfax, packed up and moved to England. For Washington there was never any question of moving. He was a Virginian, not an Englishman. However, like many others, he hoped the rumblings of war could be stilled.

In late August, Washington went to Philadelphia. He was chosen to be one of Virginia's seven delegates to the First Continental Congress. The Congress was called to bring representatives of all thirteen colonies together. This was no small achievement. The colonies jealously guarded their individual rights and privileges. Their views about government, religion, business, and other issues varied a great deal. At other times they had dealt separately with England. But now alliances were shifting. The members of the Congress hoped that if the colonies spoke with a united voice, perhaps King George III and Parliament would listen.

Washington was in Philadelphia for six weeks, saying little, but listening a great deal. There he met other colonial leaders, including John Hancock, John Adams, and Benjamin Franklin. In the end, the Congress sent a "Declaration of Rights and Grievances" to England. It didn't do any good.

When Washington returned to Virginia, he was elected to head its militia. In the past, the militia served only to protect the colony from Indians and the French. But a new enemy was looming. There was a time when anyone suggesting that the American colonies would go to war against Great Britain would have been laughed out of town. But no one was laughing now.

6
The Revolution Begins

Tension and anger was growing in every colony, but in Massachusetts they ran especially high. By early April 1775, they reached dangerous levels. British spies reported that colonists were stockpiling cannonballs and other ammunition. Why would they do this, if not for a fight? And when would they decide the fight should start?

The British commanders in Boston under Sir Thomas Gage did not fancy waiting around like sitting ducks. They decided to act. On April 18 Gage ordered 700 British soldiers from Boston to march to Concord, twenty-one miles away. Their goal was to confiscate the gunpowder and cannonballs that had been collected. They had no legal right to do this. The gunpowder and cannonballs were private property. But the British plan was to take the ammunition now and worry about legal rights later.

The countryside, however, was warned of their coming. In response, a group of about seventy Lexington Minutemen gathered on their town green. When the British arrived, they ordered the Minutemen to disperse. The Minutemen didn't like being ordered around. Still, they were badly outnumbered. Dispersing seemed like the only logical thing to do.

Then someone fired a shot. A Minuteman? A British soldier? No one ever knew for sure. But one shot followed another. In only a few moments, eight Minutemen lay dead. Ten more were wounded. The British didn't stay to count the

The Battle of Lexington, the first battle of the Revolution.

losses for themselves. They just continued on to Concord.

There they met with a much larger force of Minutemen from surrounding towns. After several hours of fighting, the British Army turned back. Colonists fired at them from behind stone walls and trees every step of the way back to Boston. In all, 247 British soldiers and 88 colonists were either killed or wounded.

News of the battles of Lexington and Concord reached Mount Vernon on April 27. Washington had just finished adding another wing to the house. In a few days he was planning to leave for Philadelphia and the Second Continental Congress, which was scheduled to start on May 10. Washington was hoping that the differences with England could be resolved without violence. Now it was too late for that.

The mood in Philadelphia was angry and defiant. The delegates were breaking British law simply by meeting, but they didn't care. They had many complaints. This latest incident at Lexington and Concord only further showed how badly the British government was acting. King George III was not treating them like loyal subjects. They were being asked to dance like puppets while he pulled their strings.

While the Congress debated what aid to send to the rebellious colonists in Massachusetts, more news arrived. The Green Mountain Boys from Vermont, a force led by Ethan Allen, had captured Fort Ticonderoga from a small British garrison. The fort, on the western side of Lake Champlain between New York and Vermont, once was an important post. The attack was made under the impression that the fort still controlled the route south from Canada. The fort, though, turned out to be in terrible condition. However, it did contain valuable military supplies.

With the air thick with talk of war, the Congress authorized the formation of the Continental Army. There was no money for arms or clothing or other supplies, but at least it was a start. The next question was, who should lead this army?

It was a difficult situation. The most experienced military leaders in the colonies were all British officers. They were not likely to join the American cause. This left only a handful of colonial candidates.

Washington was already serving on several military committees for the Congress, but he did not put himself forward as a candidate. His experience was real, but limited. He had never commanded cavalry or artillery. The little he knew of tactics concerned fighting in the wilderness. He had never faced well-drilled troops across an open field.

Still, Washington had two crucial qualifications. First, he was someone everyone could agree on. Other candidates had more passionate backers, but they had many enemies, too. Washington did not. Second, he was a southerner from Virginia. The northern delegates recognized how important this was. So far, much of the conflict had taken place in New England. If a New Englander was chosen to lead the army, southerners might then decide that the conflict did not concern them — and withdraw their support. Therefore, a southern leader would not only lead the army, he would also help maintain the loyalty of the southern colonies.

On June 16, Washington was offered the position. Whatever his doubts, he accepted with characteristic determination. In his formal acceptance, he said:

> *Tho' I am truly sensible of the high Honor done me in this Appointment, yet I feel great distress from a consciousness that my abilities and Military experience may not be equal to the extensive and important Trust: However, as the Congress desires I will enter upon the momentous duty & exert every power I Possess In their Service for the Support of the glorious Cause. . . .*

Washington also added that he wished no salary from the appointment. If he were reimbursed for his expenses, that would be enough.

While there was certainly honor in becoming Commander in Chief, there was much risk as well. The prospect of war with England was not promising. The English Army had far more men, resources, and experience. The English Navy was the finest in the world.

Washington was well aware of these facts. But he did not expect the fighting to last very long. Any war, even one favoring the British, would involve many deaths and much expense. He assumed that once George III saw how stubbornly the colonists were resisting, the king would change his policies.

The colonists didn't reckon, however, with the stubbornness of their king. While several of his ministers sympathized with the colonists, they did not have enough influence. The king did not plan to give in to a bunch of colonial upstarts.

Neither would the British commander in Boston, General Gage. On June 17, he ordered an attack on the colonial army digging in on Breed's Hill and Bunker Hill in Charlestown. The colonists, though, stood their ground in a battle that included barrages from British ships in the harbor. Both sides suffered heavy losses before the British won.

This battle was fought while Washington was starting on his way to Boston. His progress was slowed by speeches and receptions given in his honor. Washington could not afford to skip these occasions. Although it was important that he reach his army, he also needed to draw more support to the rebel cause. Many people had not decided which side to support. The sight of the bold general on his white horse might help to convince them.

Washington finally arrived in Cambridge, Massachusetts, on July 2. He already knew about the battle at Breed's Hill. Although the colonists had lost, he was pleased that they had fought well. It was encouraging that a ragtag band of soldiers could stand up to seasoned British troops, even in defeat.

Washington's first duty was to inspect the 16,000 colonial troops under his command. These men were mostly from various local militias around New England. The soldiers made a sorry sight. Their clothes were ragged. Many were barefoot. Everyone was in need of a bath.

To deal with the situation, Washington issued several orders:

All Officers are required and expected to pay diligent Attention, to keep their Men neat and clean. . . . not more than two Men of a Company [should] be absent on furlough at the same time, unless in very extraordinary cases. . . . No person is to be allowed to go Fresh-water pond a fishing or on any other occasion as there may be danger of introducing the small pox into the army. It is strictly required and commanded that there be no firing of Cannon or small Arms from any of the Lines, or elsewhere, except in case of necessary, im-

mediate defense, or special order given for that purpose.

As his army began to clean up, Washington began organizing and drilling his troops. The brightest spot in the long months of work came in December, when Martha arrived from Virginia. She wanted to be with George, and there was no one at home for her to care for. Patsy had died in 1773, a victim of one of the many illnesses that marked her seventeen years. And Jackie, who had recently married, was busy with his new life.

George was the one who needed her. She was his confidant, the one person with whom he could share his complaints and worries. It was the first of many winters they would spend together, separated the rest of the year by war.

During that fall and winter, Washington began planning a new campaign. He could not afford to leave the British blockaded in Boston — that would use up too many of his men. Nor could he simply depart with the army. That would leave the British free to follow behind him. For better or worse, he needed to drive the British out of Boston.

On the British side, General Gage was replaced by Sir William Howe, but little else changed. Howe, like so many British commanders, refused to take the Continental Army seriously. He therefore carelessly failed to fortify Dorchester Heights, a strategically important site just south

*British General
Sir William Howe.*

of Boston. On March 4, 1776, Washington launched a surprise attack and took control of the heights. He then added another surprise, displaying cannons that were brought overland hundreds of miles from Fort Ticonderoga.

The British ships in the harbor and the soldiers in town now faced the prospect of dodging cannonballs whenever Washington saw fit to fire them. Under the circumstances General Howe at first planned an attack on the heights, but a passing storm scuttled the attempt. Unwilling to risk any further losses, he ordered the British to leave Boston on March 17.

The colonists jeered and waved as the British warships sailed out of Boston Harbor. The first round of fighting went to Washington, but the real war had just begun.

7
Years of Fire and Ice

The retreating British sailed from Boston to New York City. The situation there was very different from the one they had just left. New York held thousands more British troops and more ships as well. Also the geography of Manhattan and Long Island, with its wide rivers and long coastline, underscored the strength of the British Navy.

Nonetheless, Washington moved his men to New York and prepared to fight again. But here his early luck ran out. Throughout the fall of 1776, at Brooklyn Heights and Harlem, and along the Hudson River, the inexperienced Continental Army was badly defeated. Among Washington's mistakes was his assumption that his men would act as he did in battle, keeping their heads clear

General Washington discussing strategies with his Council of War after the Battle of Long Island.

and refusing to panic. But the barefoot farmboys, who had joined the army as a lark after spring planting, were bewildered by pitched battles. They were not trained for advancing and retreating as a single unit. And they were unprepared to stand their ground while their friends died around them. There were isolated instances of colonial steadfastness, but they were too few to stem the British advances.

These early defeats were not all Washington's fault. He had problems getting supplies, and some of his officers refused to follow orders. But as the man in charge, Washington took the blame for everything. After a while men in the Congress, and even in Washington's own command, began to wonder if the right man was leading them.

For his part, Washington did not waste time worrying about his image. He concentrated on the war at hand. The fighting around New York was his direct concern. Following his latest defeats, the British were advancing into New Jersey. These defeats were not a total loss. Washington learned an important lesson from them. If he tried to fight this war according to British rules, the British would win.

The colonists had two advantages working for them: They had better knowledge of the countryside, and they had the freedom not to fight in the usual way. In Europe, armies generally faced each other in the open. The battles were expected, almost scheduled. The two sides manuevered here and there, and when the dust cleared, one side had won and the other had lost.

At first, Washington was forced into fighting these tactical battles in New York. Now he remembered what he had seen while serving under General Braddock twenty years before. The British troops had been confused by the French and Indian ambushes. They had frozen when facing a foe who didn't play by their rules. It was then that their rigid discipline became a weakness instead of a strength.

By December, the Continental Army had retreated all the way to the Pennsylvania side of the Delaware River. From this relatively safe position, Washington plotted his next move. General Howe, believing the war was all but over, returned to New York. However, he left behind strong forces in Trenton and Burlington, New Jersey. The British, imagining themselves in Washington's cold and wet shoes, expected him to sulk or despair for the winter.

But Washington did neither. Since the British did not think he would take any bold action, that was clearly what he must do. In mid-December he took his remaining 6,000 men and crossed the Delaware at night. The men fought with the bitter cold as ice floes battered their small boats. It was a daring move, and one that just barely succeeded.

On the night of December 25, Washington surprised the British troops at Trenton. These professional soldiers were Hessians from Germany. They had been celebrating Christmas all day and were in no condition for battle. After some confused fighting in the streets, the Hessians surrendered. The Continentals captured much arms and ammunition and took 1,000 men prisoner.

When news of this battle reached the British general Cornwallis, he marched on Washington's position with 8,000 troops. After a brief skirmish, Cornwallis broke off the fight. There was no need to hurry foolishly. He could wait until the next day "to bag the old fox."

But waiting until the next day to fight again was the expected thing to do — and so Washington did something else. That night was again very cold. Soldiers on both sides huddled in their blan-

Washington crossing the Delaware.

kets. The British could see that the colonists were building up their campfires. They are as cold as we are, thought the sentries.

That was probably true, but the Continentals weren't sitting around thinking about it. After building up their campfires, they stole away at Washington's command, detouring around the British force. At dawn they attacked three unsuspecting British regiments at Princeton. These regiments had felt perfectly safe behind the protection of Cornwallis's army. Now they fled or were taken prisoner. Once again Washington captured many needed supplies. And then, before Cornwallis could catch up to him, he disappeared into the countryside.

It looked like the "old fox" would not be so easy to bag after all.

The victories at Trenton and Princeton bought Washington and the Continental Army some time. A final defeat no longer seemed quite so near. But little else had changed. Supplies of clothing, food, and ammunition were still lacking. The summer before, the soldiers laughed about their bare feet and torn shirts. During the winter of 1776–77, the lack of shoes or heavy coats was no longer the subject of jokes.

The next spring and summer brought a number of British victories. The most important one was the capture of Philadelphia in September 1777. The Congress itself was forced to retreat as the British took control of the city. The only good news for the colonies came in October at Saratoga, New York. There, a force of roughly 15,000 Americans under General Horatio Gates defeated British General John Burgoyne and his 5,000 men. Washington himself was not involved in this battle. Although he was Commander in Chief, he could not personally supervise all the fighting. Also, communications on horseback were much too slow for him to guide every campaign. Other generals who technically served under him made many decisions on their own. In this case, Burgoyne's force had come down from Canada intending to join up with the army of Sir Henry Clinton in New York. Instead, Burgoyne ended up surrendering his army to Gates after suffer-

*British General
John Burgoyne.*

*American General
Horatio Gates.*

ing heavy losses. This important victory ended the threat of a British army marching south from Canada to divide the colonies in half.

It also gave General Gates a swelled head. His victory owed much to Burgoyne's foolish stubbornness in pressing onward despite several setbacks. Gates, however, conveniently ignored this fact. As far as he was concerned, his triumph was the greatest of the Revolution so far. Washington had nothing to compare with it. Perhaps the Congress would soon realize that Gates should be running the northern campaign by himself. Washington could still run the southern campaign, of course. In fact, if Washington should be removed from his position as Commander in Chief, who better than the hero of Saratoga to take his place?

Other high-ranking army officers and some members of the Congress were still critical of Washington. These men opposed him for different reasons. Some had always objected to his qualifications for the role of Commander in Chief. Others were either impatient with the slow progress of the war, or ambitious for themselves.

The threat to Washington intensified when the Board of War, which supervised war operations, was reorganized with his opponents in control. Washington dealt with this situation coolly. He realized that his responses must be cautious. Too many public squabbles between American leaders might cause public opinion to shift against their cause. The Continental Army could not afford this. It needed all the support it could muster.

In December 1777, Brigadier General Thomas Conway was promoted to Major General by the Congress and made Inspector General of the army. Washington was displeased because he knew Conway was among those who strongly opposed him. But he remained patient, refusing to create an incident that his foes might use against him. He let his critics know that he was aware of their views, but that was all. He waited them out.

The problem for Washington's foes was deciding on their next step. They were not united by any single person, and they each had their own ambitions and goals. They were unanimous in their dislike for Washington, but they could agree about little else. As the months passed, they continued to bicker. Soon, they were so busy fighting among themselves that they stopped being a threat to Washington at all.

Meanwhile, the Commander in Chief had more immediate concerns. The British, under General Howe, settled in Philadelphia for the winter of 1777–78. Howe, his officers, and his men lived in comfort there, taking over whatever homes and buildings they needed. And many people in Philadelphia still favored the British side. These Loyalists, as they were called, welcomed the British advance.

Washington and his men had nowhere as pleasant to turn to. The bedraggled army — 11,000 men — gathered at an old forge twenty miles from Philadelphia. They planned to spend the next few months in this cold and cheerless place.

Valley Forge was not an established camp. The soldiers had to build crude log huts themselves. Food was scarce, and there was a shortage of tools and nails. The men did the best they could.

As the Commander in Chief, Washington had access to a fieldstone house where he could have been fairly comfortable. But he wouldn't stay there at first. While the huts were being built, his men were sleeping in tents. Washington slept in a tent, too. This gesture meant a lot for the army's morale. The bond growing between Washington and his men would prove to be very important in the hard times ahead.

The huts, although an improvement over the tents, had their own problems. They were drafty and damp, a good place for infections to spread. Many men fell ill. There was also a shortage of soap. As they got dirtier, more and more of them became sick. Even the healthy ones itched terribly as they shivered in the cold.

It was hard, very hard, for the soldiers, who were former farmers and craftsmen, to sit around miserably when they knew warmth and food were waiting for them back in their homes. Those homes might be hundreds of miles away, but they could cross that distance in a few days. At Valley

Forge they had no idea how long their suffering would continue.

But there were more than hunger pangs at stake. Many of the men had signed on for short periods of time. They were not likely to re-enlist with an army that could not keep their stomachs from grumbling and their toes warm. If the situation did not improve, Washington might lose much of his army before spring came.

One letter from Washington to his supply officers on February 15, 1778, reveals the seriousness of the situation:

I am constrained to inform you, that the situation of the Army is most critical and alarming for want of provision of the Meat kind. Many of the Troops for four days and some longer, have not drawn the smallest supplies of this article. They have been on the point of dispersing and without the earliest releif, no address or authority will be sufficient to keep them long together.

One happy note for George was the appearance of Martha in early February. She had again come north from Mount Vernon to be with her husband. The two small rooms they shared together, one of which George used for his office, were a great change from the comfortable surroundings at Mount Vernon. But Martha didn't complain.

She bustled with energy. Like the general, the general's wife also set an example. Martha helped to care for the sick soldiers and organized social functions to brighten some of the long and dreary evenings.

The long winter was also relieved a bit by the appearance in March of Baron Friedrich Wilhelm von Steuben. The baron was a former drillmaster from Prussia in central Europe. Training soldiers to march in step, to break into difficult formations on command, was his life's work. Von Steuben had met Benjamin Franklin in Paris, and Franklin encouraged him to help the colonial cause.

Von Steuben spoke German and very little En-

Baron Friedrich Wilhelm von Steuben, center, with American troops and General Washington, right, at Valley Forge.

glish, but his enthusiasm and dedication were easily understood by all. Despite the language barrier, he and Washington got along very well. Von Steuben enjoyed his work. He threw himself into the job of turning the ragged Continentals into a professional fighting force. He started with small groups, and when they learned to fight as a unit, to react to the unexpected without panic, he sent them off to teach others. In this way the whole camp was soon practicing in earnest.

As the buds opened and the birds returned from the south, the Continental Army began to shape up. It had survived its battle with the weather. Now it was time to face the British again.

8
The World Turned Upside Down

Before there was any more fighting to be done, Washington received important news in May 1778. The French at last decided to officially recognize the rebellious colonists as a new American government.

From the beginning, the French secretly sent supplies to the colonial cause. Still bitter over the Treaty of Paris in 1763, France welcomed the chance to help embarrass the British. Unofficial aid, though, was not the same thing as formal recognition. There, the French were cautious. They did not want to risk publicly supporting the losing side. However, the American victory at Saratoga made them reconsider. Maybe this colonial uprising was going to amount to something after all.

The French decision to enter the war was crucial to the Revolution's success. It boosted the morale and stature of the new American government. It also distracted the British from concentrating on the colonists alone. Most important, it gave the colonists access to a real navy. The French fleet was a force the British could not afford to ignore.

The French admiral, the Comte François Joseph Paul de Grasse, sailed his fleet to Newport, Rhode Island, and anchored there. Washington pleaded with him in letters to bring his ships into the war directly. The admiral refused. He was willing to fight, but not simply because Washington wanted him to. He would not risk his ships in uncertain encounters. So he waited for the right moment to act.

Meanwhile, Sir Henry Clinton, now the British commander for North America, was ordered to send 8,000 of his men to fight the French directly in the Caribbean. Obviously this meant 8,000 fewer soldiers to fight the Americans. Many of these men came from the British Army in Philadelphia. Once they were gone, Clinton feared that his remaining smaller force could be surrounded by a combined American and French attack. And so, without a further shot being fired, he abruptly decided to lead his army back to the safety of New York.

Washington was still headquartered at Valley Forge when he got the news. He might have been content to lead a parade through the liberated Philadelphia, but he recognized a greater opportunity. If he acted fast, he could cut off part of the retreating British force. Clinton was not moving only his army. He was transporting 1,500 wagons of cannons and other supplies of war. Transporting everything was going to take time. Washington held several staff meetings to discuss strategy. Some officers, led by General Charles Lee, urged caution. Others, such as Nathanael Greene and Anthony Wayne, were ready to fight.

Washington finally ordered a quick march to intercept the British. By the end of June, he had led six brigades around the British supply train. They stood between the British and the New Jersey shore.

As senior officer under Washington, General Lee received command of the striking force. The fact that he thought the whole plan was stupid didn't seem to matter as much as military protocol. As the ranking officer, the job was his. But when his men went into battle, they went on their own. He gave them no leadership.

The Battle of Monmouth might still have ended in an American victory had Lee just continued doing nothing. But having done that for a while, he suddenly ordered his force to retreat. This action threw the Continental Army into such confusion that the British were able to drive the Americans back.

Washington at the Battle of Monmouth.

The retreat was fast becoming a rout. Officers and common soldiers were staggering in the heat. Among them was the young Frenchman, the Marquis de Lafayette. In the midst of this disaster, Washington rode up on his white horse. Lafayette later wrote that Washington personally stopped the retreat by riding up and down the line shouting encouragement to his men. The chance for a victory had been lost, but Washington's actions prevented a disaster.

Although Lee's behavior bordered on treason, and he was later court-martialed, it was not the only traitorous act of the war. In September 1780, Major General Benedict Arnold came close to turning over the fort at West Point, New York, to the British. This was no ordinary fort. If the British were to extend their control up the Hudson River from New York City all the way to West Point, they could seriously interrupt the flow of men and supplies passing between New England and the southern colonies.

The plan failed because Arnold's British contact, Major John André, was caught traveling behind American lines. As Washington wrote to the Congress of the incident:

> *I do not know the party that took Major André, but it is said it consisted of only a few Militia, who acted in such a manner upon the Occasion, as does them the highest honor and proves them to be Men of great Virtue. They were offered, I am informed, a large sum of Money for his release and as many Goods as they would demand, but without any effect.*

Arnold himself escaped to live out his life in England. André was shot as a spy.

While Washington was fighting traitors around him and the British over the next hill, he was also waging a difficult battle trying to keep men adequately supplied. Again and again, he wrote the Congress for money and materials. The winter of 1779–80 was almost as hard as the one at Valley Forge. In the following months, the situation worsened. Individual states were not delivering

The American Major General Benedict Arnold.

goods as promised, and the Congress was doing little about it.

In January 1781, unhappy soldiers, many from the Pennsylvania company, staged a mutiny. While Washington was sympathetic to their needs, he condemned their actions:

The aggravated Calamities and distressed that have resulted from the Total want of Pay for nearly twelve months, the want of Clothing at a severe Season, and not unfrequently the want of Provisions, are beyond description. The circumstances will now point out much more forcibly what ought to be done, than any thing that can possibly be said by me on the subject.

Negotiations ended the mutiny, but the settlement was expensive. Twelve hundred men were discharged and allowed to return to their homes.

Other soldiers saw this as an opportunity for themselves. A second mutiny began, this time by troops from New Jersey. Washington moved quickly. Whatever sympathies he may have felt for these offenders, he believed even more strongly in loyalty and military discipline. He ordered the mutineers surrounded. When they surrendered, two of their leaders were immediately executed.

There were no more mutinies after that.

Fortunately, the British were having their own troubles. In 1779, Spain had joined the war effort as an ally of France. Holland had declared war on England, too. Other European countries, including Denmark, Russia, and Prussia, were banding together to put pressure on the British.

As powerful as England was, it could not afford to fight so many countries at once. British ministers meeting with their American counterparts were prepared to offer almost anything but independence. Had they done the same ten years earlier, the Revolution never would have started.

Even as the British negotiated, their armies pressed for new advantages. In the south, they cut off Georgia from the other colonies. Having cut one colony off, the British looked for other places to do the same. General Cornwallis landed more than 7,000 men at Yorktown in Virginia.

This map shows the direction of the war as it reached its conclusion.

Cornwallis' route ∘∘∘∘∘∘
Washington and Rochambeau ———
French fleet (from the West Indies) — — —

His plan was to march through Virginia, making another cut between the colonies.

Washington was not about to let this happen. Hurried discussions passed between him and the French high command. Finally, the French ships from Newport sailed south, blockading Chesapeake Bay outside Yorktown. Meanwhile Washington led 5,700 Continentals south from New York. They were joined by 3,100 members of the Virginia militia, and a French army of 7,000 men. To keep the plan a secret, Washington did not even inform the Congress until he was already under way.

71

Washington skillfully placed the men at different points to prevent any British advance. The British Army had plenty of time to fortify their own position, but that was all they could do. They couldn't go anywhere. And with the French ships bottling up Chesapeake Bay, there was no hope of being rescued by sea. The danger that Sir Henry Clinton foresaw in Philadelphia revealed itself a few hundred miles further south. The British were trapped. As Washington tightened the ring, they retreated more and more. Finally on October 17, Cornwallis sent a message asking for a halt to the fighting. Washington's reply began:

I have had the honor of receiving your Lordships letter of this date.

British General Cornwallis surrendering to General Washington.

An ardent desire to spare the further effusion of Blood will readily incline me to listen to such terms for the surrender of your Posts of York & Gloucester, as are admissable.

Cornwallis agreed. On October 19, almost 8,000 British troops marched out of Yorktown in defeat. They walked between rows of American and French soldiers standing at attention. Cornwallis himself, embarrassed and humiliated, did not appear at the surrender ceremony. The British band, searching for an outlet for their astonishment, played a popular song of the time — "The World Turned Upside Down."

The war was almost over.

9
Winning the Peace

As pleasing as the Yorktown victory was, Washington could not just sit back and put his feet up. British fleets continued to control most of the important American seaports. The British Army, even without Cornwallis's force, still numbered more than 10,000 men. If England wanted to keep the war going, it could still turn things around.

But continuing the war was not what England wanted. The Yorktown defeat was too much for the British government to absorb. Some ministers resigned. Others, who were friendlier to American interests, took their place. They approached Benjamin Franklin in Paris and asked about terms for peace.

Meanwhile Washington received sad personal

news. His stepson, Jackie Custis, had died. It was a tragic end to a disappointing life. Jackie was not a source of pride to his family. Spoiled by both parents, he was lazy, without ambition. He never made anything of his life, even after his marriage. Most recently he had become a civilian aide to the army at Yorktown. It was there that he became ill, probably with typhus, a disease that struck many in the army camps. He died on November 5, 1781.

Washington returned to Mount Vernon for the funeral. Under other circumstances he would have enjoyed a few days of quiet at home. But with Jackie's death hanging so heavily over the family, it was not a restful visit.

Even at Mount Vernon, though, Washington continued to direct the war effort. Keeping the Continental Army properly prepared was not easy. If the British began new attacks the following spring, his men would be ill-prepared to fight back. In addition, many of them had not been paid in months. How long would they continue to fight if the Congress showed them so little respect?

The fault was not only with the Congress. Although the colonies had formally united in March 1781, under the Articles of Confederation, they still jealously guarded their individual rights. One of these rights concerned the power to raise money. The Congress did not have this power;

the states had kept it for themselves. And so far, at least, they showed no interest in giving the Congress the money for army pay.

In May 1782, Washington received a letter from Colonel Lewis Nicola. The colonel was fed up with the money situation. He suggested that perhaps the country would be better off if Washington simply became king.

This was not an impossibility. As the leader of the army, Washington was the most powerful man in the colonies. Many of his men felt a stronger loyalty to him than they did to the country itself. If Washington wanted, he could have set himself up as a new King George. Some people would have objected, but their objections would have been swept aside. History was filled with national heroes who set themselves up to rule after their campaigns ended. Also, the colonists were accustomed to having a king. Most of them would have cheered Washington on and looked forward to his reign.

For Washington, though, this was not a decision to wrestle with. His mind was uncluttered by schemes and ploys. As he had stated before, and as he would state again, he was committed to the establishment of a free republic. He wrote back to Nicola at once:

With a mixture of great surprise and astonishment, I have read with attention the sentiments you have submitted. . . . I am much at a loss

*to conceive what part of my conduct, could
have given encouragement to an address. . . . If
I am not deceived in the knowledge of myself,
you could not have found a person to whom
your schemes are more disagreeable. . . .*

Nevertheless, Washington gravely understood
the reasons behind Nicola's suggestion. The
grumbling in the army was not simply going to
disappear. If the Congress did not do something
soon, there would be trouble.

A year went by between the surrender of the
British at Yorktown and the signing of a prelim-
inary peace treaty. Even Washington, who had
been cautious about believing in the peace pro-
cess, could feel the tensions ease. There was more
time to tend to his personal life. He wrote to his
cousin, Lund Washington, who was overseeing
the running of Mount Vernon. And he wrote to
other relatives, including his nephew, Bushrod.
Washington enjoyed philosophizing to young
people. As he wrote:

*Be courteous to all, but intimate with few,
and let those few be well tried before you give
them your confidence. True friendship is a
Plant of slow Growth, and must undergo and
understand the shocks of adversity before it is
entitled to the appellation.*

*Let your Heart feel for the afflictions and dis-
tresses of every one, and let your hand give in*

proportion to your Purse. . . . But that it is not every one who asketh, that deserveth Charity: All however are worthy of the inquiry or the deserving may suffer.

Among the deserving who were still suffering were Washington's men. Although the army passed the winter of 1782–83 in relative comfort, unrest remained among the officers. If the country was treating them so poorly now, what chance would they have for fair treatment once peace was achieved? Perhaps they should not disband, even if ordered to, until their claims were met.

Washington attempted to head off such sentiments with a written general order, but written words were not enough. In the end, he realized he must speak to his officers in person. On March 15, 1783, he stood to address them. They must resist, he told them, the folly of taking rash action that would "lessen the dignity, and sully the Glory you have hitherto maintained."

Washington spoke well, in his usual calm manner, but the officers were not satisfied. When were they going to be paid? The Congress had been making empty promises to them for years. They were not convinced it was ever going to act.

As Washington listened to the grumbling, he remembered a letter he received from a congressman. The officers might find it reassuring. He took the letter from his pocket.

Washington called for his men's attention.

Then he stared at the letter for a moment. The handwriting was small and cramped. It was hard to make out.

The officers waited for him to speak. As Washington hesitated, they wondered what was wrong.

Finally, Washington took out a pair of eyeglasses. Few in the gathering had ever seen him wearing them. "Gentlemen," he said, as he put them on, "you must pardon me. I have grown gray in your service, and now find myself going blind."

This modest statement melted the officers' resolve. Their general had suffered as they had, endured the hardships they had, and maybe others that they knew nothing about. Many of the soldiers wept. They no longer really cared about the congressman's letter. Where Washington led, they would follow. They would do as he asked and wait for their pay.

In March 1783, news of the signing of the Treaty of Paris with England reached America. A few weeks later France signed her own treaty with England, officially bringing peace to all. Much of the army was disbanded in the next few months, although Washington stayed on to await the British departure from New York. That was finally accomplished on November 25, 1783.

With that event behind him, Washington's sense of duty was satisfied. On December 4, he met for the last time with his officers at Fraunces Tavern in New York City. It was hard for any of them to speak, much less to eat or drink. Washington silently embraced each one in turn, and then left for the waterfront.

Washington headed south to Annapolis, Maryland, where the Congress was meeting. In various towns along the way he was honored for his achievements. There were more dinners and balls in Annapolis, but finally Washington made his final speech to the Congress as Commander in Chief. His statement was short, touching upon the great events in which they had all played a part. His last words revealed that, at fifty-one, he imagined his public life to be over.

Washington bidding farewell to the officers of his army, at the Old Tavern in New York City, December 4, 1783.

Having now finished the work assigned me, I retire from the great Theatre of Action; & bidding an affectionate farewell to this August Body under whose orders I have so long acted, I here offer my Commission & take my leave of all the employments of public life.

Washington returned his commission to the president of the Congress. The Commander in Chief was again a Virginia planter.

10
The Reluctant Politician

The end of the war did not put an end to the former colonies' problems. In fact, their problems were growing. While the war was in progress, regional differences and jealousies were hastily put aside. Ironically, the coming of peace made it safe to start arguing again.

The biggest issue, the one that controlled all the others, had to do with power. Who was going to have it? The Congress? Each state? And what kind of power was it going to be? The power to tax? The power to make laws?

For the moment, though, these questions did not concern Washington. He happily returned to Mount Vernon, and he had every intention of remaining there. Martha was at his side, and the two young Custis grandchildren, Nelly and Jack, kept the house from being too quiet or reserved.

After eight long years tied to the fortunes of war, Washington again became a country gentleman. The house needed to be renovated and expanded, and he set those plans in motion. His main attention, though, focused on revitalizing his estates. Lund Washington had watched over Mount Vernon the best he could, but he was not the perfectionist his cousin George was. The farms had sustained many losses during the war years, and George was eager to restore them.

Despite his valiant efforts, though, Mount Vernon would never be a really thriving plantation. The land was not that fertile, and there were water shortages and various insects to deal with. Another financial drain was the growing number of slaves. The slave families just kept growing, and Washington, unlike most slave owners, refused to sell slaves and break up families (unless the slaves were willing). In time, his views shifted even more. It was not enough to make the slaves comfortable or treat them with some kind of respect. His current feelings were expressed in a letter to Robert Morris of Philadelphia:

I can only say that there is not a man living who wishes more sincerely than I do, to see a plan adopted for the abolition of [slavery] — but there is only one proper and effectual mode by which it can be accomplished, & that is by legislative authority. . . .

Unfortunately, he saw little chance of that happening soon.

Although Washington hoped to return to the world as he knew it before the war, this was not possible. Times had changed. Before the Revolution, the upper classes in Virginia maintained close ties to England. The war naturally upset those ties. Those families who had remained most loyal to England found themselves uncomfortably isolated in this new independent America. Many of them moved to England rather than make the adjustment.

And Washington, of course, was not the same, either. He did try to think of himself simply as a Virginia planter. As he wrote to a French officer and friend:

I am at length become a private citizen of America, on the banks of the Potowmac; where . . . free from the bustle of a camp & the intrigues of a Court, I shall view the busy world . . . with that serenity of mind, which the Soldier in his pursuit of glory & the statesman of fame, have not time to enjoy. I am not only retired from all public employments; but I am retiring within myself & shall tread the private walks of life with heartfelt satisfaction.

But he remained a national figure to the rest of the country. Visitors flocked to Mount Vernon.

Some were people he knew already, friends from the war like the young Marquis de Lafayette. Others just wanted to meet the famous general, or paint his picture, or borrow money from him. Washington was cordial and generous to almost everyone. He fed them, their servants, and their horses. He was the perfect host.

In September 1784, Washington headed again toward western lands in present-day Pennsylvania and Ohio. He was still fascinated by land speculation. He wandered happily about, investigating the paths of rivers and likely sites for settlements.

The states, however, were wrestling with many things besides westward expansion. The country at this time was far from being a group of united states. Under the Articles of Confederation, each former colony printed its own money and charged different taxes. Meanwhile the Congress, which was supposed to be governing the country, had to depend on donations from the states to fund anything.

Money was a problem in other ways, too. In 1785, state taxes in Massachusetts rose to about a third of a farmer's income. In 1786, after taxes were raised again, many farmers there fell into debt and were evicted from their property by the courts.

One farmer, Daniel Shays, once a captain in the Revolution, led a band of 500 angry farmers who temporarily closed some of these courts. His force grew to 1,200 men before Shays' Rebellion, as it was called, was defeated in a battle at Springfield.

There were problems abroad as well. The Treaty of 1783 gave British Loyalists in America the right to regain any property or funds confiscated from them during the war. Most of the states, though, acted very slowly to obey this provision. In response, the British, who were supposed to evacuate their forts in Niagara, Detroit, and other places, refused to do so. If the Americans were not going to abide by the treaty, neither would they.

This confusion over authority could not continue forever. The states wanted to do business with other countries, but other countries were hesitant. Who should they make trade treaties with — individual states or the country as a whole?

Clearly, there was a real need for a strong central government to oversee the many issues that crossed state lines. In September 1786, a general trade convention was called for in Annapolis, Maryland, but only five states showed up. Still, some of its delegates convinced the Congress to call for another convention in Philadelphia the following May. The announced purpose of this meeting was to revise the unworkable Articles of Confederation.

Washington was reluctant to attend this new

convention. He would have been content to remain in a comfortable chair at Mount Vernon and advise younger men from there. But his prestige and experience were needed for the convention to succeed. Of course, he could simply have refused to go. That would have meant shirking his duty, however, something he would not do.

Washington arrived in Philadelphia a day before the convention was scheduled to begin on May 9, 1787. It was not until May 25, though, that everyone was ready to start. The other fifty-four delegates had many different reasons for being there. Some were eager to see a strong national government emerge from the proceedings. Others were determined to keep this from happening. The oldest delegate was eighty-one-year-old Benjamin Franklin. The youngest was twenty-six-year-old Jonathan Dayton of New Jersey.

Washington served as president of the convention, but he did not speak publicly during the deliberations. The leaders decided quickly to do more than simply revise the Articles of Confederation. They wanted to go further, to make an entirely new constitution. They kept their discussions secret, though, even posting men at the door to keep eavesdroppers away.

The delegates decided that under a constitution, the federal government would be divided into three branches — the executive, the legislative, and the judicial. Each branch would have

Washington presiding over the Constitutional Convention.

distinct powers. This division of responsibility would keep the government in balance. No one branch would be able to dominate the others.

Establishing the makeup of the legislative branch, the Congress, proved to be the biggest hurdle. The problem centered on the issue of representation. The larger states wanted the number of congressmen for each state to be based on population. The smaller states, afraid of being constantly pushed around, proposed a system in which each state would have the same representation.

Eventually a compromise was reached. Roger Sherman of Connecticut suggested the creation of a two-house Congress. Membership in the lower house, the House of Representatives, would be based on population. Membership in the upper house, the Senate, would be the same for all states.

The executive branch was going to be headed by the president. His term of office was settled on four years, after discussion in which it ranged from three years to life. A few delegates, including Benjamin Franklin, wanted the general population to elect their president. Most of the delegates, though, did not trust ordinary voters to make such a big decision. Instead, they decided that each state would appoint a board of electors. This Electoral College would then vote for a president.

The delegates finally finished their business on September 17, 1787. Washington marked the occasion with the first mention of the convention in his diary:

The business being thus closed, the Members adjourned to the City Tavern, dined together and took a cordial leave of each other — after which I returned to my lodgings . . . and retired to meditate on the momentous w[or]k which had been executed, after not less than five, for a large part of the time Six, and sometimes 7 hours sitting every day, [except] sundays & the ten days adjournment . . . for more than four Months.

Nine of the thirteen states needed to approve the Constitution before it would be accepted. Delaware was the first — in December 1787. By the following summer, though, almost all the other states had voted for it. The Constitution was now the law of the land.

11
President Washington

With the Constitution in place, the states busied themselves electing their senators and congressmen. On February 4, 1789, the Electoral College made their decision.

Who would the first president be?

George Washington was the unanimous choice. Nobody else had the respect and trust of the various factions in the Congress. Nobody else had the necessary prestige in all thirteen states. And nobody else gave the new nation the respectful image it needed to do business with other nations as an equal.

Washington accepted the call back to public office with some regrets. The former major in the Virginia militia, who once happily campaigned for responsibilities far beyond his years and ex-

Washington receiving the announcement of his election to the first presidency of the United States.

perience, was now an older and wiser man. At fifty-seven, his ambitions were largely satisfied. And he had his share of aches and pains. At Mount Vernon he could rest or complain as he saw fit. As president, his personal comfort would often need to be put aside. The vice-presidential choice, John Adams, did not yet have enough national support, and no one else had the necessary backing.

Still, he never truly questioned accepting the job. Washington recognized how fragile the strength of the new Constitution was. If he declined the presidency, the debate over choosing another candidate might rip the union of states apart.

The Constitution called for the first president to be sworn into office on March 4, 1789. But that date passed without the votes having been officially counted. Washington finally learned of his election on April 14 from Charles Thomson, the Secretary of Congress. In response, Washington read a statement in which he said:

I am so much affected by this fresh proof of my Country's Esteem and Confidence that silence can best explain my gratitude. While I realize the arduous nature of the Task which is imposed upon me, and feel my own inability to perform it, I wish however that there may not be reason for regretting the Choice — for indeed all I can promise is only to accomplish that which can be done by an honest zeal.

Washington left for New York City within a few days. The city already had a hospital, a library, a college, and a prison. Now it was going to become the capital of the new nation. On April 30, Washington was inaugurated before a large crowd after traveling in a parade. He promised to execute faithfully the office of President, and to preserve, protect, and defend the Constitution. Afterwards he went indoors to give his inaugural address to the Congress. It was a brief speech, one in which Washington expressed the hope that:

. . . the foundations of our national policy will be laid in the pure and immutable principles of private morality; and the preeminence of free Government be exemplified by all the attributes, which can win the affections of its citizens and command the respect of the world. . . .

Putting all this into practice was a lot of work, and Washington's first year in office was especially busy. He approved the Bill of Rights, guaranteeing freedoms of speech, religion, and other personal rights, and the Judiciary Act of 1789, which created a national court system.

Unlike the presidents who followed him, Washington had no examples to follow. Realizing that every presidential action established some kind of precedent, he tried to make his every action above reproach. Although he was offered housing by old friends, he insisted that the government rent housing for him so that the president would not be obliged to a private citizen. Further, Washington never belonged to any party or aligned himself with a particular group. The president, he thought, should not be led by any petty or partisan concerns. He should simply be president of all the people.

Washington was aware that he was setting an example in little things as well as big ones. A president must look the part, he thought, and Washington favored velvet suits with gold buckles. When he traveled, it was in a coach led by four or six horses, attended by footmen. Once a week he made himself openly available to callers. At other times, callers needed an appointment. He also appeared at informal receptions the First Lady held on Friday afternoons. He stopped shaking hands, however, acknowledging formal greetings with a bow.

These receptions were more of a duty than a pleasure for Martha. The First Lady disliked having to adjust to the social pressures of New York. Some people thought the Washingtons, with their fancy carriages and servants, acted too much like royalty. Others, after enduring the President's plain receptions and dull early dinners, thought the Washingtons didn't go far enough. It was a situation Martha couldn't win. As she wrote to her niece: "... I am more like a state prisoner than anything else, there are certain bounds set for me which I must not depart from. ..." When the capital moved from New York to Philadelphia in 1791, the situation improved a little. Gradually, Martha grew more accustomed to public life and it troubled her less.

The President shared many of his wife's views, but he at least had the larger concerns of running the country. Serving under him were several men responsible for different areas of the government. Together they formed the cabinet. The Attorney General, Edmund Randolph, was the chief law

President Washington and his first Cabinet. From left to right: Washington; General Henry Knox, Secretary of War; Alexander Hamilton, Secretary of the Treasury; Thomas Jefferson, Secretary of State; and Edmund Randolph, Attorney General.

officer. Henry Knox, the Secretary of War, was responsible for the nation's defense. The two most important people, however, were the Secretary of State, who oversaw relations with other countries, and the Secretary of the Treasury, who supervised the financial policy of the country.

These positions were held by two brilliant, but very different, men. Thomas Jefferson was the Secretary of State. A native of Virginia, Jefferson had been the principal author of the Declaration of Independence when he was only twenty-six. Wary of the power of cities and organized financial institutions, Jefferson had become the leading spokesman for strong states' rights.

Alexander Hamilton was the Secretary of the Treasury. Born on the island of Barbados, Hamilton had played a crucial role in creating the Constitution. Unlike Jefferson, Hamilton was a Federalist, who wanted a strong central government. Toward this end he backed the formation of a national bank and other measures that would strengthen federal control.

The differences between the two men spilled into foreign considerations as well. Jefferson, having served as Minister to France, had many ties there. Furthermore, the recent revolution there had overthrown the French king and set up a republic. But the shifting alliances and changes in the new French government did not impress Hamilton. He recognized how important British banking and trade would be for the healthy growth of the United States. And so he favored strong ties with the English.

Although Washington tried to avoid taking sides, he favored the Federalist position on many issues. With Hamilton's guidance, a whole network of taxes and tariffs was devised and implemented. The money raised from these sources was used to pay off the national debt and run the government. Washington knew that many of Hamilton's plans benefited already wealthy financiers and businessmen, but their support helped ensure the stability of the new government.

As the end of his four-year term neared, Washington hoped that he could retire. The country was set on the proper course. Governing it could now be left to others.

This was wishful thinking. Although much progress had been made, the country was now sharply divided between Hamilton's Federalists and Jefferson's Democrat-Republicans. In fact, Jefferson resigned as Secretary of State after deciding that he could no longer support Federalist policies. About the only thing he and Hamilton agreed on was that Washington should run for a second term.

The prospect of serving another four years did not excite Washington. He was tired. He longed for the peace of Mount Vernon where his every opinion was not dissected and analyzed. Still, he-would not desert the country when it needed him. In 1792, he was easily re-elected, and the runner-up, John Adams, again became Vice-President.

Washington's first term was largely spent creating the machinery of a national government and getting it to run. Now he had to deal prominently with foreign affairs.

In 1793, war broke out between France and England. The French wanted to use American ports to help supply and refit their ships. They felt they had the right to American support under the treaty signed between the two countries in 1778.

This was a difficult problem for Washington. He well knew how much the success of the American Revolution owed to the French. And yet he was unwilling to commit the United States to the French side. The French and British were not fighting over ideals, they were fighting for territory and power.

The situation was further complicated by the French Ambassador to the United States, Edmond Genêt. When the Americans did not immediately pledge support for the French, he began traveling around making speeches. He hoped to stir up enough public support to influence the President's views. He also saw to it, against the American government's wishes, that several ships were outfitted for French use.

When Washington still remained neutral, Genêt changed his strategy. He publicly criticized the President. Washington was out of touch, said Genêt. He was not honoring the true feelings of the American people.

This tactic backfired. Genêt was not as popular as he thought, and the public's regard for Washington ran very deep. As word of Genêt's insults to the President spread, his influence fell. He was eventually recalled to France, where a new government planned to have him beheaded on the guillotine. Had Washington wanted revenge for the trouble Genêt had caused him, he could have sent him home. Instead, he allowed Genêt to stay in the United States, where the former ambassador went on to live a peaceful and uneventful life in upstate New York.

His decision to stay neutral really had nothing to do with Genêt. He was convinced that involvement in another war would soon tear the United States apart. For once Hamilton and Jefferson agreed, even though Jefferson's sympathies were with France. Washington finally issued a Proclamation of Neutrality on April 22, 1793, in which he advised Americans to remain impartial in conflicts between other countries.

Washington would not remain neutral, though, when a revolt broke out in western Pennsylvania in 1794. Farmers there were upset over a federal excise tax on whisky. Having gone to war almost twenty years earlier because of taxation without representation, they were still unhappy with taxation — even when it came with a vote. Some of the farmers even banded together in what was called a Whisky Rebellion and attacked federal officials who came to collect the taxes.

Washington acted quickly. The nation's laws must be obeyed, even when they weren't convenient. The situation called for a demonstration of power and resolve. Washington put on his old uniform and prepared to fight. As Commander in Chief, he led 12,000 men from Philadelphia toward the rebellious western counties.

The farmers hesitated when they saw how clearly the government and the President were willing to back up their laws with force. Washington still cut an imposing figure astride his great white stallion. The ride may have been less comfortable than it was twenty years before, but his expression was as resolute as ever. Washington was sending a message. He would order troops out even against American citizens if they threatened the country's peace and stability. The Pennsylvania farmers got this message, and the rebellion stopped without any real fighting becoming necessary.

Further fighting with England, however, remained a possibility. The British still inhabited several forts they were supposed to have turned over to the United States. They were also encouraging the Indians to harass American settlers on the frontier. On the high seas, large British ships were bullying smaller American ones. Facing a shortage of sailors, British forces were boarding American ships and removing American sailors to work for them. The British claimed that these sailors were actually British deserters. Perhaps a few of them were, but most were not.

John Jay, who had earlier been appointed the first Chief Justice of the Supreme Court, was sent to England to try and resolve these problems. It was not an easy task. When Jay returned home, he had a new treaty in which the British agreed to leave the forts by 1796. The other important issues, though, were put aside to be settled in the future.

Not surprisingly, the Jay Treaty, ratified by the Senate on June 24, 1795, was quite unpopular. Even Washington thought that his minister had achieved very little. In fairness to Jay, though, there was little pressure he could put on the British. In some ways he was lucky to get anything at all.

Although the Jay Treaty with England was not especially favorable to the United States, it did prompt Spain to move forward with a treaty, too. Pinckney's Treaty, negotiated by Thomas Pinckney in 1795, helped to define the western and southern boundaries of the United States. It formally extended the edge of the country to the Mississippi River, and gave American shipping unrestricted access to New Orleans. Both of these provisions would quicken the pace of westward expansion.

As his second term drew to a close, Washington

looked ahead to retirement. Had he wanted to, he could have been re-elected to a third term, but his health and inclinations were firmly against it. In his farewell address, Washington prepared some final words of advice to the nation. He never actually delivered this speech, but the text was published in many newspapers. In it, he expressed his views on several topics. Most important, he cautioned against becoming too closely allied with other countries.

> *The great rule of conduct for us, in regard to foreign Nations, is extending our commercial relations, to have with them as little political connection as possible. . . .*
>
> *'Tis our true policy to steer clear of permanent alliances, with any portion of the foreign world. . . .*

Washington's continuing fear was that if the United States was pulled into a war, the fragile union of states might quickly come apart. He understood, of course, that some wars might be unavoidable. However, the country should avoid alliances because they might pull it into unnecessary conflicts.

In the election that fall, John Adams won a narrow victory over Thomas Jefferson. The Federalists' power was weakening, but for the moment they were still in control. On March 3, 1797, the day before Adams's inauguration, Washington pardoned ten men who were convicted of treason for their part in the Whisky Rebellion. It was one of his last official acts.

The elder statesman returning to Mount Vernon a few days later could take pride in his accomplishments. Under his leadership, an untried government designed on paper had prospered in its first eight years. Some problems, though, were beyond his control. Party politics, something Washington tried to avoid, had already reared its head. And the threat of war was always present. Nevertheless, Washington's judgment, balanced by his caution, gave the new government time to work. Although he never entertained such a grand thought, the nation would always be in his debt.

12
Retirement

Washington left for home on March 7, 1797. His refusal to run for a third term showed his confidence in the new nation. No one person was crucial to the country's survival, Washington was saying. His retirement was proof of that.

As the Washingtons traveled south, there were dinners and receptions every night in their honor. George and Martha patiently endured them all, even though they were eager to get home. Among the places they passed through on the way to Mount Vernon was the unfinished Federal City — as the former president continued to call it. Other people referred to the city by its new name — Washington.

The condition of Mount Vernon was, as usual

after one of Washington's long absences, not good. There was much to repair and set right. A fireplace mantel was almost falling off the wall. Several beams needed replacing. Only a short while before, Washington had been writing to kings and generals. Now he wrote of more everyday things, as in this letter to his secretary.

I have got Painters at work in order to prepare my room for furniture which is expected; but I find I have begun at the wrong end, for some joiners work . . . ought to have preceded theirs, as the fixing of the chimney pieces ought also to do.

Martha was busy, too. More than 200 trunks and crates were shipped home from Philadelphia. Their contents had to be emptied, sorted through, and put in their proper places before the house would truly feel like home again. As she went about her work, Martha probably sighed in relief and pleasure. There would be no further moving. She and the general were home for good.

Washington described his daily routine in a letter to Secretary of War James McHenry. He wrote that his morning began at sunrise, when he checked to see that his workers were beginning their duties. After breakfast at about seven o'clock . . .

I mount my horse and ride round my farms, which employs me until it is time to dress for dinner at which I rarely miss seeing strange faces, come as they say out of respect for me — Pray would not the word curiosity answer as Well? And how different this from having a few social friends at a chearful board? The usual time of Sitting at Table — a walk — and Tea, brings me to the dawn of candle light . . . but when the lights are brought I feel tired & disinclined to engage in this work, conceiving that the next night will do as well: the next comes & with it the same causes for postponement & effect & so on.

This will account for your letters remaining so long unacknowledged — and having given you the History of a day, it will serve for a year. . . .

Despite the informal description of his daily life, Washington was still in touch with government affairs. He was particularly troubled by the way the latest French government (which had changed several times since the French Revolution in 1789) had received the current American representatives. For example, in 1797, certain French officials demanded bribes in return for negotiating. These officials were never named. They were known only as X, Y, and Z. But when news of the XYZ Affair became public, it caused a great scandal. In 1798, relations between the two countries became so strained that the possibility of war emerged.

Under the circumstances, President Adams asked Washington to again accept command of the American army. He was the only figure that the different political factions would happily accept. Washington was reluctant to take up such a role, but as he wrote to the Secretary of War:

> *Under circumstances like those accompanied by an actual Invasion of our territorial rights, it would be difficult for me, at any time, to remain an idle spectator under the plea of Age or Retirement. . . .*

Under the threat of battle, Washington agreed to spend some time in Philadelphia at the end of the year. There he helped to plan for enlarging the army on short notice. He also found time to write to his New York dentist about his false ivory teeth (the only teeth he had), which had caused him much discomfort. It's not certain whether or not the dentist was able to help him, but at least the French decided against an American war and Washington was able to go home.

There were struggles at home, too. His granddaughter Nelly was pleasant company, but his grandson Jack was proving to be lazy and troublesome. He dropped out of college and returned to Mount Vernon. Washington sent his grandson a note requesting that he study well, appear at meals, and generally make good use of his time. Washington was not hopeful that his grandson would change his habits, but he was willing to give him the chance.

Some quiet pleasures still lay ahead. In January 1799, the Washingtons celebrated their fortieth wedding anniversary. The years gone by had certainly been full of surprises, but both bride and groom remained happy with the partner each had chosen.

The rest of the year passed quickly. In February, Washington celebrated his sixty-seventh birthday. In July, feeling old age creeping upon him, Washington made his will. He was the last surviving member of his immediate family. His mother had lived till 1789, observing most of his triumphs, though appreciating them less than other people. She was always more concerned about herself than she was interested in George.

Washington's will contained many conventional and traditional instructions. Among them, though, was a more unusual one. Washington directed that after Martha's death, his 300 slaves were to be freed. Furthermore, the young slaves were to be educated first, and the oldest ones, who could no longer work, were to be cared for until their deaths.

On December 12, 1799, Washington went for his usual ride around his farms. The weather was stormy, but he ignored it. The cold and snowy ride lasted several hours. He came home exhausted, his throat scratchy, and he quickly developed laryngitis. Under the care of local doctors, he gargled with a mixure of molasses, vinegar, and butter. Spanish fly, a preparation of dried beetles, was also placed on his throat in the hopes that it would draw the sickness out.

None of this seemed to help. His continuing illness stretched over the next two days. Martha was constantly at his bedside, but she could only watch and wait. Three doctors were consulted, and each thought something different was wrong. As was the medical custom, a vein was opened to let some of Washington's blood out. This was

George Washington on his death bed.

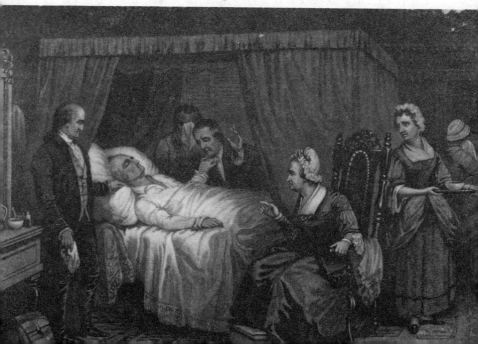

done four times in all, leaving the former president weaker and weaker.

Late on December 14, he called his secretary to his bedside, and hoarsely gave him instructions. "I am just going. Have me decently buried, and do not let my body be put into the vault in less than two days after I am dead."

A few minutes later he was gone.

The news of Washington's death sent the whole country into mourning. Martha missed him most of all, and she spent the remaining three years of her life living quietly at Mount Vernon, surrounded by her family.

Many speeches were made and articles written about Washington at his death. He had been that rare man of history — both a conquerer and a statesman — and the people recognized him for it. Of all the words used to honor him, though, the most famous were uttered by the Governor of Virginia, Henry Lee. As Lee declared, Washington truly was "first in war, first in peace, and first in the hearts of his countrymen."

Index

Page numbers for illustrations are in italics.

114

About the Author

Stephen Krensky was born in Boston, Massachusetts, only a few miles from where George Washington took command of the Continental Army. He is the author of thirty books for children, including *Children of the Earth and Sky* and *Who Really Discovered America?* Mr. Krensky lives in Lexington, Massachusetts, with his wife, Joan, and their sons Andrew and Peter.